HSE
Health & Safety
Executive

MANUAL
HANDLING
in
DRINKS
DELIVERY

HSE BOOKS

CONTENTS

PREFACE

This booklet has been written in consultation with a working party representing
the major employer organisations and trade unions in the drinks industry; and with local
authority associations and the Health and Safety Executive (HSE). It follows requests for
advice from the industry and sets out information on the responsibilities of employers,
persons in control of premises and employees under Health and Safety at Work etc Act,
and the Manual Handling Operations Regulations. The guidance is *not* mandatory but the
suggestions and examples are based on good practice currently in use.

INTRODUCTION

1   Accidents resulting in injury during the production and distribution of drinks are a cause for serious concern:

❏   In production, *one third* of the accidents arise from the manual handling activities;

❏   In delivery, nearly *two-thirds* of the accidents arise from manual handling.

Injuries to the hands and feet are common, and damage to the back can have long-lasting effects which can be career-threatening. Some injuries are the result of a single incident, but many disabling back injuries come from repeated lifting of heavy loads over several years. The costs of these accidents can be high in human as well as financial terms; and recent research suggests that the true costs are substantially greater than the insured loss.

This booklet is intended to assist the following people to reduce the risk of injury to delivery and other staff:

❏   managers and supervisors in small breweries and soft drinks producers;

❏   those responsible for the transport, distribution and delivery of drinks;

❏   those in charge of premises such as hotels, pubs, off-licences and other shops;

❏   employees and safety representatives.

2   The Management of Health and Safety at Work Regulations 1992 require employers to assess all the risks to the health and safety of their employees and anyone else who may be affected by the work activity. The employer can then decide what steps need to be taken to reduce the risks. If this general assessment identifies risks from manual handling operations, then the detailed requirements of the Manual Handling Operations Regulations 1992 should be followed. These and the accompanying Approved Code of Practice set out the framework for reducing the risks to the health and safety of employees from manual handling:

❏   AVOID the need for hazardous manual handling (ie with a risk of injury) as far as is reasonably practicable;

❏   ASSESS the risk of injury from any hazardous manual handling that cannot be avoided; and

❏   REDUCE the risk of injury from hazardous manual handling as far as reasonably practicable.

3   The first part of this booklet gives general guidance to employers. The second part is guidance to those in control of premises and the third part is for those who actually have to carry or move the loads. It is written largely in the terms of delivering beer and soft drinks to the pub, but the same principles can be applied to a wide variety of delivery activities.

4   The Regulations refer to the lifting, handling or moving 'loads' and in the drinks trade these can include:

❑   casks and kegs of beer, lager or cider;

❑   cases and crates of beer, soft drinks, wines and spirits;

❑   shrink wrapped trays of cans;

❑   gas cylinders, detergents in drums, dispense equipment.

Some of these containers will have also to be returned to the depot or manufacturer when empty, or part-empty ('ullage').

ADVICE TO EMPLOYERS

Assessments - general

5   An assessment of manual handling is needed: if the operation includes the transporting or supporting of a load (including the lifting, putting down, pushing, pulling carrying or moving of the load) by hand or by bodily force; *and* a risk of injury exists; *and* the manual handling operation cannot be avoided entirely. It is the *combination* of the weight of the load, the frequency of handling and the location that make it likely that injury could occur through manual handling. You should look for all reasonably practicable opportunities to eliminate or reduce the amount of manual handling. However, the variety of the work means that deliveries may stay a predominantly manual task for the foreseeable future.

6   It is important to remember that *the assessment should be a relatively simple process to identify risks; the major effort should be devoted to reducing those risks.* Where the risks can be easily explained, or where they are low, there is no need to record the assessment. Where you need to keep a record, it need contain only the significant findings. Where you have a number of identical sites, or a number of workers doing similar tasks, it may only be necessary to make a common assessment, and not one for each site or each worker. Assessments can also be built up from a number of standard components if the activities involve similar tasks or equipment and can be done on a sample basis.

Starting the assessment

7   Criteria for typical risk assessments of premises and safe systems of work include:

❑   common factors to the activity, eg similar weights and shapes of containers, and common vehicles used for the delivery. A table of weights for most containers etc used is at Appendix 5;

❑   variable factors covering the characteristics of each delivery location, especially those where the storage area is not at ground floor level. Factors include the height for lifting or lowering full and empty containers, manoeuvring storage space and headroom available, condition of floors and stairs.

8   Where these factors may create a risk, it will be necessary to improve the situation by making changes or repairs, and possibly the provision of handling aids. These will need to be considered where they can help to reduce the risk of injury because of the nature of the load to be handled. Training requirements for delivery and other staff should then be drawn up to reduce the possibility of injury, bearing in mind the common and variable factors at each location.

9   In some cases you will be well aware of the nature of the premises and the problems: the same sort of deliveries may have been made to the same pub for many years. However, when renovations are planned the opportunity should be taken to upgrade the storage areas as well as those the public will use.

Reducing the risk

❑   Is there information on the weight and balance of loads?

❑   Can the size/weight of the load be reduced? What more needs to be done to make the operation safer?

❑   Has a 'safe system of work' been developed, ie is there a planned system for handling loads (particularly for large ones such as casks and kegs, both on the level and between levels) which is intended to reduce the risk of injury?

❑   If a 'safe system of work' has been instituted, is it being monitored and kept up to date?

❑   Has adequate equipment (eg hoists, barrows, ropes, hooks, skids etc) been provided and maintained?

❑   Has adequate training been given and the individual's competence and capability to carry out the task been assessed?

❑   Is there a regular review of reports of injuries and absences or damage that could indicate continuing or new problems?

10   Although the Regulations do not specify who should do the assessment, they do require that it be suitable and sufficient. It therefore follows that the assessment should be done by a competent person, who has the necessary knowledge and experience. In most cases you should be able to do the assessment in-house but there may be occasions where external advice on manual handling procedures could be beneficial. Contributions from the employees should be encouraged as they are likely to have more experience of the tasks than anyone else. In summary, you are responsible for ensuring that the assessment is suitable and sufficient.

11   If an existing 'drop' or delivery has no specific or unusual hazards (eg delivery of small quantities of soft drinks to a ground floor shop) the assessment should be simple and straightforward. Where problems are identified, for example delivery above or below ground level, large quantities or unusual access, a more detailed assessment of the premises may be required.

12 Risks will depend on the working environment, the task, the load and on individual capability, and will determine the probability of an accident or injury occurring. A further indication of whether injury/ill-health is foreseeable may also be gained from the company/ group sickness, accident or incident history. Evidence of damage to property and equipment may also indicate problem areas.

Assess the workplace

13 The assessment for a particular 'drop' needs to consider all aspects of the working environment including the unloading point, the storage area or cellar and the route between the two. It will need to take account of factors such as road traffic, safety of the public and distance to the place of storage. It is also important to assess lighting, steps, stairs, headroom, floors and entrances so that the safest route is taken. With experience, this may have to be reassessed. Appendix 4 suggests a way in which this assessment could be recorded.

Consider the method

14 Mechanical handling devices, powered and non-powered, are available to ease the movement of kegs, casks, cases and cylinders. 'Mechanical assistance' does not necessarily mean 'powered assistance'. Devices include:

❑ barrows, trolleys or sack trucks;

❑ lifting devices (powered or non-powered) for placing casks on stillages;

❑ hoists/lifts from pavement to cellar - a number of purpose-designed devices are now available;

❑ cranes, tail lifts etc on the lorry.

Where these are already available for use, they should be considered with the assessment. All work equipment needs to be maintained and assessed for mechanical safety and other risks.

Consider the task/load

15 Employers and employees should be aware of the duties under the Road Traffic Act and Regulations for the vehicle load to be properly secured while travelling, and ensure that loading procedures take account of these.

16 At the depot/warehouse the loading of the vehicle needs careful planning in order to reduce the need for rearrangement at the delivery points and to avoid unnecessary unloading onto the vehicle's offside. Safe access to the load on the vehicle is necessary, and arrangements should be made for a working space on the vehicle's bed.

17 Lifting heavy containers manually may lead to injury. A safe system of work should be prepared if it can be foreseen that topping, ie placing one full or part-full container (cask or keg) on top of another, is to be carried out manually. This should set out the procedures to be adopted, either by team handling or by using mechanical or other suitable aids. However, topping of containers weighing over 70 kg should not be required unless mechanical aids are used as part of a safe system of work.

18 The safe system of work should not require topped containers (including those on saddle pallets) to be unloaded straight to ground level from a vehicle by hand, unless the top of the topped container can be reached from the working position, eg beside a low-level deck vehicle, in order to keep control of the container.

19 The assessment then needs to consider the task, the loads and personnel involved. This will mean taking account of the types, weights and quantities of containers and packages that have to be delivered, the frequency of handling/delivering and any specialised handling equipment available.

20 Any risk from storing, stacking or moving of containers and packages will have to be carefully assessed and safe systems developed which take account of these. Some form of mechanical handling equipment may be appropriate.

21 The removal of partly empty containers (ullage) can also give rise to a risk of injury because of the unknown weight etc so a suitable procedure should be drawn up and included in any assessment.

Training

22 Although mechanical handling equipment and an improved working environment have major parts to play, training of all delivery personnel should be undertaken to ensure that these measures are effective in reducing the risk of injury from manual handling.

23 You should develop and implement a manual handling training programme which

incorporates the company's safe system of work and good handling techniques appropriate for the trade.

24   Ideally, the training programme should be developed in conjunction with employees' safety representatives, and further input from medical staff and ergonomists could be considered. Video material could be useful as a training aid. You should ensure that your employees clearly understand how the manual handling operations have been designed to safeguard their health and safety.

25   All employers, including those who use part-time, temporary or agency staff who may have to handle or lift loads, should arrange for suitable basic training to be given. The training should be assessed and reviewed as necessary. This basic training should take place before any employee undertakes any manual handling duties where there is a risk of injury. There should be further 'on-the-job' training given where appropriate.

Training programme

26   A typical training programme given by a suitably trained and experienced instructor containing the elements set out below should be implemented.

Theory

❑   Information on accident statistics, particularly cases of back, hand, foot and other injuries to the body in the industry and their causes, in the company/group;

❑   Good handling technique;

❑   The company 'safe systems of work': why they have been developed and how they operate;

❑   The weights of typical loads which will be handled and information on the centres of gravity.

Practical instruction

❑   Use of handling aids and personal protective equipment;

❑   Implementation of safe systems of work;

❑   How to deal with difficult and unfamiliar loads;

❑   Good lifting techniques;

❑ How to deal with a variety of working environments;

❑ The importance of good housekeeping and keeping a tidy work area;

❑ The importance of employees reporting to their employers any injury or illness which might affect their physical ability to carry out manual handling operations.

Refresher training

27 This should be conducted at regular intervals as necessary: to advise on developments in the use of lifting aids; to update on good handling techniques; and to prevent 'bad habits' creeping in. It may be necessary to give an update on the weights and handling procedures for any new product when it is introduced.

28 It may be useful to keep a record of the training given to each employee. Similar records of any reassessment carried out and of monitoring done will be useful to ensure that systems of work are being adhered to. Employees should be consulted as part of any review of training or systems of work.

Protective clothing

29 Suitable protective clothing should be supplied if it is necessary, eg overalls, safety shoes/boots, gloves, aprons etc. Suitable fluorescent or reflective clothing should be supplied for use where deliveries are carried out in bad light or adverse weather conditions.

ADVICE TO THOSE IN CONTROL OF PREMISES

The term 'cellar' used here includes the place where beer, barrels, kegs and similar containers are stored, whether underground, at ground level or at any other level. The same requirements can be applied to the stock room of a shop or store.

30   The reduction in the risk of injury from manual handling depends to a great extent on the design and maintenance of the premises and equipment where the goods are delivered. This is the responsibility of the person in control of those premises. There is also a duty on employers to co-operate in the performance of their duties under the Health and Safety at Work Act and Regulations. This is important when improved handling methods are being planned. The safe movement of stock from the store to the point of sale should also be considered.

General

31   The place to which the load is to be carried should be assessed, and steps taken to eliminate, as far as reasonably practicable, risks to people delivering, moving or storing goods. You should ensure the following:

❑   The yard or other parking place is free from obstruction as far as possible;

❑   Safe entrances and exits from the building are available for the delivery drivers;

❑   The delivery route is properly maintained and kept clear;

❑   The route is kept free from water (so far as possible), ice or other materials (eg food scraps) likely to make the floor slippery;

❑   There is adequate lighting;

❑   There is sufficient space to allow safe manoeuvring of containers. This may mean that deliveries/returns may need to be made more frequently to avoid holding large stocks;

❑   There are some situations (eg small, low ceilinged cellars or several flights of stairs) where manual handling operations may be difficult. It may be necessary to change the size/weight of containers delivered to avoid unreasonable risks to the people who have to move them. Alternatively, mechanical aids (eg mobile stackers) should be considered;

❑   Any animals on the premises should be under proper control so they do not become a risk to those carrying out the delivery.

32   You should also identify and mark damaged packages, or partially full containers (ullage) which have to be removed and where there is a risk to the people who have to handle them.

33   The employers of delivery personnel may have to visit the premises in order to carry out the assessment required under the Manual Handling Operations Regulations regarding their own employees, and this should be facilitated. The Management of Health and Safety Regulations require co-operation in reducing risks where there is overlapping control.

Underground storage

34   If there is an opening in the floor inside or outdoors, such as in the pavement, you should ensure that the flap cannot accidentally close. People not engaged in the process should be kept away from the cellar opening while delivery is taking place, and suitable bars, chains or other barriers should be provided, maintained and used to prevent falls. Cellar openings are also found in the bar area, and precautions should be taken to prevent bar staff or the public from falling down cellar steps or openings.

35   Where appropriate, you should consider the benefit of providing mobile or fixed mechanical handling equipment, whether powered or non-powered. This should take account of the numbers and weights of the containers to be moved and also the physical constraints of the building.

36   Where fixed slides or skids are still used in which ropes have to be employed to control descent, it is the duty of the person in control of the premises to ensure that the

equipment is maintained in good order. It is particularly important that the surrounding area is kept free from boxes, crates or other obstructions.

Overground storage

37   Where deliveries are to be made to storage above ground level consideration should be given to the provision of powered lifting equipment where the numbers and weights of the containers indicates a potential risk of injury. Where this is not possible it is particularly important that the stairway is in good repair, adequately lit and of sufficient width to allow safe movement, eg where two people are required to carry the container/package. It may be necessary to limit or vary the unit size or quantities supplied at each delivery where no mechanical device is installed and there is a risk of injury to employees.

ADVICE TO EMPLOYEES

38 Before you leave the depot ensure that all handling equipment intended for use at deliveries is in good condition.

39 Before you move off you should ensure that your vehicle and load are not unsafe in the terms of the Road Traffic Act and Regulations.

40 The security and stability of the load between drops must be maintained. It is important to drive appropriately as the load diminishes or changes throughout the day.

41 Ensure that each delivery is being made to the proper access point identified in the assessment.

42 Ensure that the delivery access point is clear and that during the delivery members of the public are not likely to be put at risk.

43 Heavy items should be safely unloaded from the vehicle in the way described in the company's written safe system of work.

44 Follow the laid-down methods of dealing with common hazards, which may include:

❑ If a curtain sided vehicle is used, look before opening the curtains to see if the load has moved against the curtain. Always pull the curtain with you until you are sure that the load inside is stable.

❑ Always use the correct method of climbing onto and off the vehicle. Do not jump off the vehicle. This is a common cause of injury.

❑ Where topping of containers is done it is necessary to use the safe system of work which has been established. Full containers over 11 gallons (70 kg) should not be 'topped' unless mechanical aids are used. The written safe system of work should also cover unloading. The safe system of work should be recorded.

❑ The safe system of work should not allow topped containers to be unloaded straight to ground level (see paragraph 18). Where containers are topped they should be securely chocked or otherwise restrained to keep them stable during travel.

❑ Damaged and broken pallets should be put to one side and removed from use back at the depot.

❑   Wherever possible, you should create enough space on the deck of the vehicle to handle containers safely.

❑   Handle broken glass with care, and dispose of it safely.

45   Before starting to unload, check there is a clear and safe route to the storage area. It is possible that circumstances have changed, eg there are obstructions in the way steps have been damaged or lighting has failed. The problem should be raised first with a person in charge of the premises, but if the problem cannot be resolved it should be reported back at the depot using the system the company has for reporting, recording and reviewing hazards or defects. Take sufficient time to work carefully; rushing it may cause an accident to yourself or others.

Alcohol consumption

46   Drivers will be aware that there are legal limits to drinking and driving. Draymen and delivery staff should remember that it impairs your judgement and can lead to accidents to yourself and others. Deliver alcohol - do not drink it at work.

APPENDICES

APPENDIX I   CHECKLIST FOR EMPLOYERS

47   Have you surveyed the manual handling tasks to see which ones are likely to cause injury?

48   Have you organised the work in ways to eliminate or minimise manual handling operation where the weight, frequency or location can be a cause of injury?

49   Have you minimised the risks by providing mechanical aids, and ensured no new risks have been introduced?

50   Can the containers be improved, so they are easier to handle? Can grips be provided? Can you improve the external state of the containers? Can containers be marked to show how or where to hold them? Are they likely to be made slippery by wet weather?

51   Has the necessary personal protective equipment been provided?

52   Is all handling equipment etc properly maintained and accessible for use?

53   Can the vehicle, premises or task be redesigned to reduce bending, twisting, stretching, carrying for long distances, frequency of handling? Can jobs be rotated to avoid repetition and constant exertion? Is proper allowance made for rest pauses?

54   Can the premises be made safer by widening gangways, removing obstructions, keeping floors clear and providing better lighting and non-slip flooring materials?

55   Has allowance been made for individual characteristics of the workforce?

56   Is a training programme in place? Is its effectiveness being maintained? Are records being reviewed regularly?

57   How many tasks require special strength or fitness? Is this taken into account in employment selection or job allocation? Are the effects being monitored?

APPENDIX 2   CHECKLIST FOR THOSE IN CONTROL OF PREMISES

58   Have you made an assessment of the workplace to identify manual handling risks to both your own employees and other persons engaged in delivery activities? How can the risks be reduced? Have you considered the safety of members of the public?

59   Is it possible to make arrangements for mechanical handling aids to be provided, eg hoists or lifts, conveyors, trolleys, skids or chutes?

60   Can the access to the storage area be made safer by widening gangways, removing obstructions, keeping floors clear and providing proper lighting?

61   Is the cellar area or store room being maintained in a safe condition? Is there sufficient space to move containers and packages into their final storage point? Are empties suitably stored or removed so as not to cause obstruction?

62   Can ordering and stocking patterns be changed to avoid storage areas becoming overcrowded?

APPENDIX 3   CHECKLIST FOR EMPLOYEES

Delivery crews

63   Before you leave the depot each day, check your delivery handling equipment, which may include barrows; dropping bags (dump bags, pigs); dropping rope and hook; skids and caseboards; and sheet. Use the safe systems of work in which you have been instructed including the safe use of the equipment provided, and report any defects as soon as possible.

Handling of containers

64   At the 'drop' delivery crews should:

❏   wear the protective clothing provided, eg gloves, aprons, protective footwear, and use ropes, dropping bags etc when appropriate;

❏   be aware of other vehicles, pedestrians and the condition of the ground when loading and unloading;

❏   position the dropping bag correctly when unloading containers;

❏   prevent containers from rolling uncontrolled;

❏   move all containers into the cellar area one at a time, ie do not drop several barrels together;

❏   warn anyone in the cellar when a container is being passed to them - be sure that whoever is below is ready to receive it before you pass the container down;

❏   when delivering below ground and there is no hoist or similar equipment, always use the dropping rope or other approved method;

❏   separate damaged containers for return to depot;

❏   take special care to ensure that no bottles protrude above the cases and ensure that each case is properly seated into the one below;

❏   use the barrow for moving cases or can packs over a distance;

❏   ensure that cases and can packs are properly loaded on the barrow before moving;

❏   hold the top case when tilting the barrow to prevent the stack collapsing;

❑ take care when moving, especially at corners. In wet weather, plastic wrapped cartons may become slippery and therefore require extra restraint;

❑ take care when handling shrink wrapped goods. The wrapping may tear if it is used as a handle;

❑ when removing empties, watch out for broken bottles and place any broken glass in waste bins. Do not place broken glass in plastic return sacks unless it is first wrapped;

❑ on your return to the depot, report all damaged or missing equipment so that it can be repaired or replaced before the next delivery or round.

All workers

65 Wherever you are, you should handle loads with care; and, where they are appropriate, follow the recommendations set out in paragraph 64.

APPENDIX 4 EXAMPLE OF AN ASSESSMENT CHECKLIST FOR 'THE DROP'

This checklist suggests how you could start to record an assessment of the features of a pub, shop or store that would affect the handling of loads in and out of the building. For the purposes of the Manual Handling Operations Regulations, this will form *part* of the assessment, and should be added together with the factors that relate to the load, the task and individual's abilities.

Address of premises _____

_____

Section 1   Outdoor access

1   Vehicle parking. Describe parking arrangements;
    eg   on road
          off road
          customers yard
          are there any restrictions?

2   Distance from vehicle to delivery point (entrance, door, hatch)
    (a) less than 10 metres
    (b) between 10-20 metres
    (c) greater than 20 metres

3   Does the delivery route have any of the following features?
    (a) slopes
    (b) uneven surfaces
    (c) slippery surfaces
    (d) steps/stairs
    (e) other features (describe)

4   Is there a loading bay or deck?

5   Is there opportunity for lift truck or pallet truck delivery?

Comments _____

_____

_____

Section 2   Indoor access

1   Description of cellar/store (eg traditional cellar, third floor storeroom)
    (a)   If the cellar floor is not at ground level, indicate the height above/below ground
        (i)   less than 5 ft
        (ii)   between 5-10 ft
        (iii)   greater than 10 ft
        (iv)   number of floors above/below
        (v)   Is there a power operated lift/hoist available for use?

    (b)   Delivery method
        (i)   fixed chute
        (ii)   removable skids
        (iii)   lift
        (iv)   vertical/inclined cellar hoist
        (v)   other
        (vi)   Is the dropping ring in good order (if appropriate)?

    (c)   Are casks placed on stages/stillages/racks?
        Are casks placed on top of each other?
        Are devices provided for lifting them?

    (d)   Empties/ullage; removal method
        (i)   manual lifting
        (ii)   hoist/lift
        (iii)   ropes etc

2   Where loads are to be carried up/down steps or stairs, are they
    (a)   wooden?
    (b)   metal?
    (c)   stone/concrete?
    Are they in good condition?

Comments

_____

_____

_____

_____

_____

Section 3   Premises: general

1   Are cellar flaps in good condition?

2   Is the internal and external lighting sufficient for safe working?

3   Are the floors/and floor coverings in good condition?

4   Is the ceiling height at any part of the route less than 6 ft 6 ins (2 metres)?
    If so, state height and location.

5   Is the route/cellar floor kept clear?

6   To effect this delivery safely, what other requirement do you require?

Comments

_____

_____

_____

_____

Assessment of risk

Do any of the features involve a significant risk or injury?

Is the drop considered to be *high/medium/low risk* in terms of difficulties in manual handling?

What remedial steps should be taken, in order of priority?

Assessment carried out by _____

Remedial action

Action agreed _____

_____

_____ (And check that it has the desired effect)

APPENDIX 5   WEIGHTS AND DIMENSIONS OF FULL AND EMPTY CONTAINERS

	Empty weight (kg)	Full weight (kg)	Standing height (cm)	Belly width (cm)	End width kegs/casks (cm)
30 litres	9.9	40.6	35.8	39.9	39.9
50 litres	11.8	62.2	52.8	39.9	39.9
9 g aluminium	9.5	50.5	49.0	41.3	30.5
9 g steel	18.5	59.5	49.0	41.3	30.5
10 g aluminium	10.0	55.5	49.5	39.4	39.4
10 g double aluminium	19.1	64.5	52.0	39.4	39.4
10 g steel	12.3	57.7	52.0	39.4	39.4
11 g aluminium	9.1	60.0	53.3	39.4	39.4
11 g double aluminium	19.5	70.4	53.3	39.4	39.4
11 g steel (galvanised)	20.3	70.9	53.3	39.4	39.4
11 g stainless steel	12.5	63.0	53.3	39.4	39.4
Guinness 11 g					
Twin chamber aluminium	18.2	68.9	62.2	45.0	44.0
Single chamber steel	11.8	62.2	62.2	45.0	44.0
18 g aluminium	15.0	97.7	59.9	51.1	37.6
18 g wood	38.3	121.0	66.0	50.8	-
22 g aluminium	16.4	118.2	62.9	54.6	45.1
36 g aluminium	28.0	193.6	74.9	62.2	49.5
36 g wood	63.4	229.0	78.7	66.0	-

Weights and dimensions of drinks packages

Boxes and crates of bottles	Empty weight (kg)	Full weight (kg)	Height (cm)	Length (cm)	Width (cm)
12 x pint bottle	7.3	14.1	27.9	34.9	26.7
24 x 0.5 pint bottle	9.1	15.9	22.9	43.8	30.5
6 x flagon bottle	6.4	12.7	31.8	30.5	21.6
6 x soda bottle	9.5	14.5	31.8	31.8	22.2
12 x litre bottle	12.1	24.1	31.8	36.8	28.6
36 x min bottle	11.8	18.2	20.3	43.2	33.0
24 x 16 oz cans	0.2	12.3	15.2	41.9	27.4
24 x 10 oz cans	0.2	7.9	10.2	41.9	27.4
12 x 70 cl bottles, cased	-	15.0 (about)	-	-	-
CO_2 cylinder 20 lb	13.6	22.7	111.8	13.3	13.3
CO_2 cylinder 14 lb	9.1	15.5	63.5	17.1	17.1

HSE acknowledges the help of the Brewers and Licensed Retailers Association in compiling this table

APPENDIX 6   REFERENCES

Priced publications

Manual handling: Manual Handling Operations Regulations 1992: Guidance on Regulations L23 1992 ISBN 0 7176 0411 X

Manual handling: solutions you can handle HS(G)115 1994 ISBN 0 7176 0693 7

Free publications

Getting to grips with manual handling: a short guide for employers 1993 IND(G) 143L

Manual handling (pocket card) 1993 IND(G) 146L

5 steps to risk assessment 1994 IND(G) 163L

Lighten the load 1994 This pack is available from Sir Robert Jones Memorial Workshops, Units 3 and 5-9, Grain Industrial Estate, Harlow Street, Liverpool L8 4XY.
Tel: (051) 709 1354/5/6

APPENDIX 7   FURTHER INFORMATION

This guidance was prepared by the Drinks and Packaging National Interest Group of HSE. Further advice can be obtained from the National Interest Group at 59 Belford Road, Edinburgh EH4 3UE, Tel 031 247 2000 or the HSE Local Authority Unit at Rose Court, 2 Southwark Bridge, London SE1 9HF.

There are a number of other HSE publications which are appropriate to manual handling in other industries. If you would like any information about these, a full list of HSE publications may be obtained from the Information Centre at the address given on the back cover.

Printed and published by the Health and Safety Executive   C100   5/94